ASIATIC LION VS. BENGAL TIGER

BY KIERAN DOWNS

TORQUE
TM

BELLWETHER MEDIA • MINNEAPOLIS, MN

T0014900

Torque brims with excitement
perfect for thrill-seekers of all kinds.
Discover daring survival skills, explore
uncharted worlds, and marvel at mighty
engines and extreme sports. In *Torque* books,
anything can happen. Are you ready?

This edition first published in 2023 by Bellwether Media, Inc.

No part of this publication may be reproduced in whole or in part without written
permission of the publisher. For information regarding permission, write to
Bellwether Media, Inc., Attention: Permissions Department,
6012 Blue Circle Drive, Minnetonka, MN 55343.

Library of Congress Cataloging-in-Publication Data

Names: Downs, Kieran, author.
Title: Asiatic lion vs. Bengal tiger / by Kieran Downs.
Other titles: Asiatic lion versus Bengal tiger
Description: Minneapolis, MN : Bellwether Media, 2023. | Series: Torque:
   animal battles | Includes bibliographical references and index. |
   Audience: Ages 7-12 | Audience: Grades 4-6 | Summary: "Amazing
   photography accompanies engaging information about Asiatic lions and
   Bengal tigers. The combination of high-interest subject matter and light
   text is intended for students in grades 3 through 7"– Provided by publisher.
Identifiers: LCCN 2022001054 (print) | LCCN 2022001055 (ebook) | ISBN
   9781644877593 (library binding) | ISBN 9781648348754 (paperback) | ISBN
   9781648348051 (ebook)
Subjects: LCSH: Lion–India–Juvenile literature. | Bengal tiger–Juvenile literature.
Classification: LCC QL737.C23 D693 2023 (print) | LCC QL737.C23 (ebook) |
   DDC 599.7570954–dc23/eng/20220112
LC record available at https://lccn.loc.gov/2022001054
LC ebook record available at https://lccn.loc.gov/2022001055

Text copyright © 2023 by Bellwether Media, Inc. TORQUE and associated logos are
trademarks and/or registered trademarks of Bellwether Media, Inc.

Editor: Rebecca Sabelko   Designer: Josh Brink

Printed in the United States of America, North Mankato, MN.

TABLE OF CONTENTS

THE COMPETITORS

India's forests are home to some of the world's largest big cats. Asiatic lions are top cats in the Gir Forest. They **ferociously** defend their **territories**.

But Asiatic lions are not the only big cats in India. Bengal tigers are deadly **predators**. Who would win if these cats crossed paths?

Asiatic lions are a **subspecies** of lion. They live in the Gir Forest in western India. Asiatic lions have short tan or gray fur. Males have long manes around their necks.

Asiatic lions live in groups called prides. Males lead prides. Females care for young. They also do most of the hunting.

MANES

Male Asiatic lions with long, dark manes are often the healthiest. They are more likely to be noticed by females.

ASIATIC LION PROFILE

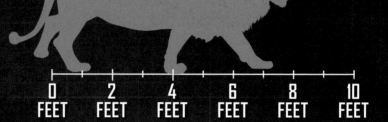

```
0       2       4       6       8       10
FEET    FEET    FEET    FEET    FEET    FEET
```

LENGTH
UP TO 8.2 FEET
(2.5 METERS)

WEIGHT
UP TO 419 POUNDS
(190 KILOGRAMS)

HABITATS

SHRUBLANDS

FORESTS

ASIATIC LION RANGE

☐ RANGE

BENGAL TIGER PROFILE

0 FEET   2 FEET   4 FEET   6 FEET   8 FEET

LENGTH
UP TO 6 FEET
(1.8 METERS)

WEIGHT
UP TO 500 POUNDS
(227 KILOGRAMS)

HABITATS

WETLANDS   GRASSLANDS   TROPICAL FORESTS   MANGROVE FORESTS

BENGAL TIGER RANGE

■ RANGE

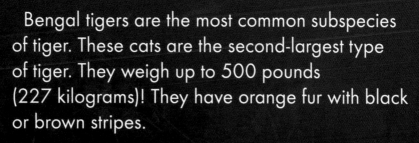

Bengal tigers are the most common subspecies of tiger. These cats are the second-largest type of tiger. They weigh up to 500 pounds (227 kilograms)! They have orange fur with black or brown stripes.

Bengal tigers live in forests in southern Asia. These big cats are **solitary** and very territorial.

SECRET WEAPONS

OUT OF SIGHT

Tiger prey cannot see orange!

Bengal tigers use their striped fur as **camouflage**. The dark stripes look like shadows and branches. This camouflage allows the tigers to sneak up on **prey**.

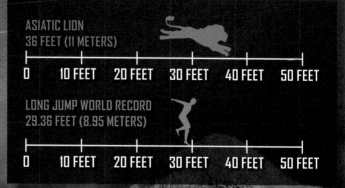

ASIATIC LION
LEAPING DISTANCE

ASIATIC LION
36 FEET (11 METERS)

| 0 | 10 FEET | 20 FEET | 30 FEET | 40 FEET | 50 FEET |

LONG JUMP WORLD RECORD
29.36 FEET (8.95 METERS)

| 0 | 10 FEET | 20 FEET | 30 FEET | 40 FEET | 50 FEET |

Asiatic lions have powerful legs. They can leap as far as 36 feet (11 meters)! They use their legs to pounce onto prey.

Asiatic lions have sharp, curved claws. They allow the lions to hold onto their prey. Their claws **retract** to stay razor-sharp.

MARKING TERRITORY WITH CLAWS

UP TO 4 INCHES
(10 CENTIMETERS)

Bengal tigers also have sharp claws. Each claw grows up to 4 inches (10 centimeters) long! **Dewclaws** sit at the back of their front paws. They help the tigers grab prey.

SECRET WEAPONS

POWERFUL LEGS

RETRACTABLE CLAWS

LARGE, SHARP TEETH

Asiatic lions have up to 30 sharp teeth in their mouths. Their large **canine teeth** rip into prey. The rest of their teeth are used to cut and slice up meat.

BENGAL TIGER

STRIPED FUR

SHARP CLAWS

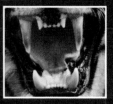

LONG, SHARP CANINE TEETH

Bengal tigers have the longest canine teeth of all big cats. Their canines grow up to 4 inches (10 centimeters) long! These sharp teeth slice through meat.

ATTACK MOVES

Female Asiatic lions hunt large prey together. Prides often begin their search at night. They quietly circle their prey so it cannot escape. Then, they take the animal down!

Bengal tigers **stalk** their prey. The tigers use their camouflage to hide in the forest. They sneak in close and attack!

Asiatic lions leap onto the backs of their prey. They dig their claws and teeth into the animal. They hold on tight as they drag their meal to the ground.

Bengal tigers attack prey with their sharp canine teeth. Bites to the back of the neck finish small prey. Bites to the throat bring a large animal down.

MEATY MEALS

Bengal tigers may eat as much as 88 pounds (40 kilograms) of meat at one time!

READY, FIGHT!

A male Asiatic lion spots a Bengal tiger hunting in its territory. The lion hides in the forest until the tiger is close. Then, the lion attacks!

The lion jumps on the tiger's back and digs its claws into the tiger. But the tiger turns and sinks its teeth into the lion's neck. The lion escapes, but it is badly hurt. The tiger won new hunting territory!

GLOSSARY

camouflage—colors and patterns that help an animal hide in its surroundings

canine teeth—long, pointed teeth that are often the sharpest in the mouth

dewclaws—special claws used for grabbing prey; dewclaws are found on the back of an animal's front paws, and they do not touch the ground.

ferociously—strongly and intensely

predators—animals that hunt other animals for food

prey—animals that are hunted by other animals for food

retract—to get pulled back in

solitary—living alone

stalk—to follow closely and quietly

subspecies—particular types of animals that exist within a species

TO LEARN MORE

AT THE LIBRARY

Downs, Kieran. *Lion vs. Cape Buffalo.* Minneapolis, Minn.:
Bellwether Media, 2021.

Krieger, Emily. *Animal Smackdown: Surprising Animal Matchups
with Surprising Results.* Washington, D.C.: National Geographic
Kids, 2018.

Sommer, Nathan. *Siberian Tiger vs. Brown Bear.* Minneapolis,
Minn.: Bellwether Media, 2021.

ON THE WEB

FACTSURFER

Factsurfer.com gives you
a safe, fun way to find
more information.

1. Go to www.factsurfer.com

2. Enter "Asiatic lion vs. Bengal tiger" into the search box
   and click 🔍.

3. Select your book cover to see a list of related content.

INDEX